FASTEN YOUR SEAT BELT

**Stats and facts • Top makes
Top models • Top speeds**

By David Kimber, Bill Gunston,
Jeff Painter, and Steve Parker

Studio Manager: Sara Greasley
Editor: Claire Lucas
Production Controller: Ed Green
Production Manager: Suzy Kelly

ISBN: 978-1-84696-205-9

Tracking number: 3233LPP1109

North American edition copyright © *ticktock* Entertainment Ltd. 2010.

First published in North America in 2010 by *ticktock* Media Ltd.,
The Old Sawmill, 103 Goods Station Road, Tunbridge Wells, Kent TN1 2DP, U.K.

Printed in China
9 8 7 6 5 4 3 2 1

All rights reserved. No part of this publication may be reproduced, copied, stored in a retrieval system, or transmitted in any form or by any means electronic, mechanical, photocopying, recording, or otherwise without prior written permission of the copyright owner.

Picture credits
(t=top, b=bottom, c=center, l=left, r=right, OFC=outside front cover, OBC=outside back cover):
Shutterstock: OFC. Cars: All images Car Photo Library—www.carphoto.co.uk, except Alamy: 8–9c. Airplanes: Corbis: 28–29, 46–47. Aviation Picture Library: 30–31, 32–33, 36–37, 38-39, 40–41. Lockheed: 42–43, OBC. NASA: 34–35, 44–45, 48–49. Motorcycles: All images Car Photo Library—www.carphoto.co.uk, except Hwithaar/Wikimedia Commons: 50–51c. Boats: Alamy: 85. Beken of Cowes: 76c, 82–83c. British Antarctic Survey: 78–79. Corbis: 74–75c, 80–81, 83t, 84c. Hawkes Ocean Technologies: 75t. John Clark Photography: 72–73c. RNLI: 90–91. World of Residensea: 88–89. Yamaha: 87t.

Every effort has been made to trace copyright holders, and we apologize in advance for any omissions. We would be pleased to insert the appropriate acknowledgments in any subsequent edition of this publication.

The publishers would like to thank Keith Faulkner of *Jane's Defence Weekly*, Richard Newland of *Fast Bikes* magazine, Jamie Asher, Sam Petter, and Tim Bones.

CONTENTS

INTRODUCTION 4

CARS

ASTON MARTIN V12 VANQUISH 6
BMW Z8 8
BUGATTI VEYRON 10
CHEVROLET CORVETTE Z06 12
FERRARI F50 14
JAGUAR XJ220S 16
LAMBORGHINI MURCIÉLAGO 18
McLAREN F1 20
PAGANI ZONDA C12 S 22
PORSCHE 911 GT2 24
TVR TUSCAN 26

AIRPLANES

AIRBUS A380 28
SR-71 BLACKBIRD 30
B-2 SPIRIT 32
B-52 STRATOFORTRESS 34
EUROFIGHTER TYPHOON 36
F-117A NIGHTHAWK 38
HARRIER 40
JOINT STRIKE FIGHTER 42
SPACE SHUTTLE 44
VOYAGER 46
X-43A 48

SUPERBIKES

APRILIA TUONO FIGHTER 50
BENELLI TORNADO 52
BUELL XB9R FIREBOLT 54
CAGIVA V-RAPTOR 1000 56
DUCATI 999R 58
HARLEY V-ROD 60
HONDA CBR1100XX BLACKBIRD ... 62
KAWASAKI NINJA ZX-12R 64
MV AGUSTA F4 SPR SENNA 66
SUZUKI GSX1300R HAYABUSA 68
YAMAHA YZF-R1 70

BOATS

CALIFORNIA QUAKE DRAG BOAT 72
DEEP FLIGHT SUBMERSIBLE 74
ILLBRUCK RACING YACHT 76
JAHRE VIKING OIL SUPERTANKER ... 78
JAMES CLARK ROSS
  RESEARCH SHIP 80
LOS ANGELES FIREBOAT NO. 2 82
NIMITZ-CLASS AIRCRAFT CARRIER .. 84
POLARIS VIRAGE TX JET SKI 86
THE WORLD LUXURY LINER 88
TRENT-CLASS LIFEBOAT 90

GLOSSARY 92
INDEX 95

Unless otherwise stated, the cost quoted refers to the time of the machine's launch.

INTRODUCTION

CARS

The fastest cars have room for a driver, a passenger, and not much else! These machines are certainly not sensible family cars—they are built for speed. They are low to the ground with an **aerodynamic** body and a powerful engine. Sports cars are admired all over the world. They are not just beautiful pieces of engineering—they are works of art.

AIRPLANES

The first airplane flew in 1903. Aviation technology developed quickly, and now millions of passengers travel by plane each year. Planes are flying faster and farther than ever before. Today, some of the most exciting new aircraft are being developed by the military.

SUPERBIKES

Motorcycles have always symbolized the freedom of the road and an escape from everyday life. The machines in this book make that escape easier than ever before. They are some of the fastest bikes in production. These are not just motorcycles—they are **superbikes**.

BOATS

All boats float on water and have a means of power and a way for the crew to control speed and direction. But the variation in boat design is immense. Some are built for short trips in safe waters, while others brave the worst weather on the open seas. The boats in this book celebrate the amazing diversity of travel by water.

ASTON MARTIN V12 VANQUISH

British company Aston Martin made its first sports car in 1914. Almost 90 years later, the **V12** Vanquish went on sale. With a powerful **engine** and a **body** made out of the lightweight metal **aluminum**, the four-seat Vanquish is one of the fastest cars in the world.

DID YOU KNOW?

In the movie Die Another Day, *James Bond drives a V12 Vanquish.*

The car has **tire**-pressure sensors, rain sensors, and even sensors that turn on the headlights when it gets too dark.

CARS

The V12 has **Formula One**-style **gearshift paddles** behind the steering wheel. You click right to change up a **gear** and left to change down.

STATS AND FACTS

LAUNCHED: 2001

ORIGIN: United Kingdom

ENGINE: 5.9L (5,935**cc**) V12, front mounted

MAX. POWER: 460 **bhp** (343kW) at 6,800 **rpm**

MAX. TORQUE: 400 ft. lb. (540**Nm**) at 5,500 rpm

MAX. SPEED: 190 mph (306km/h)

ACCELERATION: 0–60 mph (0–97km/h): 4.5 seconds

WEIGHT: 4,045 lbs. (1,835kg)

COST: $219,000

The body panels are shaped by hand to make sure the edges are perfect.

BMW Z8

The Z8 is a modern sports car with an old-fashioned look. This **roadster** is based on the beautiful BMW 507 built in the 1950s. Thanks to the enormous power of its **V8** engine, the Z8 is more than just beautiful. Without its electronic speed reducer, the top speed would be 180 mph (290km/h).

The Z8 has a safety system called **dynamic stability control** (DSC). If a corner is entered too quickly, the system stops the car from going faster and the **brakes** slow down all four wheels.

CARS

The dials are placed unusually in the center of the **dashboard**. This gives the driver a clear view of the road.

STATS AND FACTS

LAUNCHED: *2000*

ORIGIN: *Germany*

ENGINE: *4.9L (4,941cc) 32-valve V8, front mounted*

MAX. POWER: *400 bhp (298kW) at 6,600 rpm*

MAX. TORQUE: *369 ft. lb. (500Nm) at 3,800 rpm*

MAX. SPEED: *155 mph (250km/h) (limited)*

ACCELERATION: *0–60 mph (0–97km/h): 4.8 seconds*

WEIGHT: *3,494 lbs. (1,585kg)*

COST: *$118,000*

Z8 customers can choose between a hardtop or a soft-top for their roadster.

DID YOU KNOW?

The Z8's satellite-navigation system is hidden behind a flap in the dashboard.

BUGATTI VEYRON

The Bugatti Veyron is one of the most expensive **production cars** in the world, and one of the fastest. When the Veyron reaches 137 mph (220km/h), hydraulics lower the car, and its rear retractable spoiler and wing are **deployed** to help hold it onto the road.

CARS

The initials *EB* on the Bugatti badge stand for Ettore Bugatti, the founder of the company. The Veyron is named after Pierre Veyron, who won the 1939 24 Hours of Le Mans race for the original Bugatti company.

A unique aluminum alloy was developed for the interior of the Veyron to ensure that it remains shiny.

The Bugatti emblem on the large **radiator** grille was enameled by hand.

STATS AND FACTS

LAUNCHED: 2005
ORIGIN: France
ENGINE: 8.0L (7,993cc) 64-valve midmounted quad turbo engine
MAX. POWER: 987 bhp (736kW)
MAX. TORQUE: 922 ft. lb. (1,250Nm) at 2,200–5,500 rpm
MAX. SPEED: 253.2 mph (407.5km/h)
ACCELERATION:
0–60 mph (0–97km/h): 2.5 seconds
0–249 mph (0–400km/h): 55.6 seconds
WEIGHT: 4,162 lbs. (1,888kg)
COST: $1.2 million

DID YOU KNOW?

The Veyron was the world's fastest production car, until the Shelby SSC Ultimate Aero TT reached 256.18 mph (412.28km/h) in 2007.

CHEVROLET CORVETTE Z06

American car company General Motors built its first Chevrolet Corvette in 1953. It soon became the world's most popular sports car. Millions of Corvettes have been sold around the world. The reason for the car's success is simple—the Corvette is very fast but comes at a reasonable price.

DID YOU KNOW?
More than 200 of the earliest Corvettes have survived. They are now highly collectible.

In 1999, General Motors gave the Corvette a fighter-plane-style display. Speed, revolutions per minute (rpm), and fuel levels are projected onto the windshield.

CARS

This beautiful Corvette was built in 1960. Its powerful V8 engine gave a top speed of 130 mph (209km/h). The average top speed of cars at that time was only 50 mph (80km/h).

STATS AND FACTS

LAUNCHED: 1997

ORIGIN: United States

ENGINE: 7.0L (7,008cc) V8, front mounted

MAX. POWER: 505 bhp (377kW) at 6,000 rpm

MAX. TORQUE: 385 ft. lb. (521Nm) at 4,800 rpm

MAX. SPEED: 175 mph (282km/h)

ACCELERATION: 0–60 mph (0–97 km/h): 4 seconds

WEIGHT: 3,130 lbs. (1,420kg)

COST: $52,600

The Corvette comes in three body styles: **coupé** (hardtop) for cold-weather driving, **targa** (with a solid lift-out roof panel), and **convertible** (soft-top) for warm-weather driving.

FERRARI F50

Ferrari is one of the most famous makers of sports cars in the world, and the F50 is one of the most exclusive models ever built. Just 349 cars were built to celebrate the Italian legend's 50th anniversary in 1995. This incredible car is powered by a slightly less powerful version of a 1990 Formula One engine.

The F50's body, doors, and seats are made from lightweight **carbon fibers**.

CARS

Underneath the car the body is completely flat. The four tailpipes stick out through holes cut into the rear, just like a racecar.

STATS AND FACTS

LAUNCHED: *1995*

ORIGIN: *Italy*

ENGINE: *4.7L (4,699cc) 60-valve V12, midmounted*

MAX. POWER: *520 bhp (388kW) at 8,500 rpm*

MAX. TORQUE: *347 ft. lb. (470Nm) at 6,500 rpm*

MAX. SPEED: *202 mph (325km/h)*

ACCELERATION: *0–60 mph (0–97km/h): 3.7 seconds*

WEIGHT: *2,976 lbs. (1,350kg)*

COST: *$474,000*

The engine is in the middle of the F50. It powers the Ferrari to 60 mph (97km/h) in under four seconds. The car goes from 0–100 mph (0–161km/h) in only eight seconds and 0–150 mph (0–241km/h) in 18 seconds.

DID YOU KNOW?

The F50 is a very expensive car. But you still have to wind the windows up and down by hand!

15

JAGUAR XJ220S

In the late 1980s, British carmaker Jaguar decided to build a **supercar**. Jaguar called it the XJ220. In 1992, the first models were delivered to customers, costing $650,000 each. Two years later, Jaguar produced an even faster, lighter, and cheaper version of the car. It was called the XJ220S.

> **DID YOU KNOW?**
>
> In 1994, racing driver Martin Brundle reached 217 mph (349km/h) in an XJ220S. At the time, this was the fastest-ever speed recorded by a road car.

The back of the car has an enormous wing. It stretches straight across the body of one of the widest sports cars ever made.

CARS

The XJ220S was built by TWR (Tom Walkinshaw Racing). It based its design on the XJ220C cars that took part in the Le Mans race in France in 1993.

STATS AND FACTS

LAUNCHED: 1994

ORIGIN: United Kingdom

ENGINE: 3.5L (3,498cc) twin-turbo V6, midmounted

MAX. POWER: 680 bhp (507kW) at 7,200 rpm

MAX. TORQUE: 527 ft. lb. (714Nm) at 5,000 rpm

MAX. SPEED: 217 mph (349km/h)

ACCELERATION: 0–60 mph (0–97km/h): 3.3 seconds

WEIGHT: 3,439 lbs. (1,560kg)

COST: $406,300

The XJ220's aluminum body was replaced with carbon fibers to make the car even lighter. The power was also increased from 542 bhp (404kW) to 680 bhp (507kW).

17

LAMBORGHINI MURCIÉLAGO

Ferruccio Lamborghini was a millionaire tractor maker from northern Italy. Unhappy with the Ferrari he owned, he decided he could build a better car himself. In 1966, Lamborghini made the first real supercar, the Miura. In 2001, the company started selling its tenth model, the Murciélago.

The roof and the doors of the Murciélago are made of steel. The rest of the car is made from carbon fibers.

DID YOU KNOW?
The Lamborghini badge features a charging bull, a symbol of both beauty and violence.

CARS

To reverse the Murciélago, most drivers flip open a door and sit on the edge of the car. They can then look over their shoulder to see where they are going!

STATS AND FACTS

LAUNCHED: 2001

ORIGIN: Italy

ENGINE: 6.2L (6,192cc) V12, midmounted

MAX. POWER: 571 bhp (426kW) at 7,500 rpm

MAX. TORQUE: 479 ft. lb. (649Nm) at 5,400 rpm

MAX. SPEED: 205 mph (330km/h)

ACCELERATION: 0–60 mph (0–97km/h): 4 seconds

WEIGHT: 3,638 lbs. (1,650kg)

COST: $226,000

The Murciélago is easier to drive than previous Lamborghinis. It has **four-wheel drive** and a safety system that slows the car down if it starts to lose its grip on the road.

McLAREN F1

McLaren is a famous maker of Formula One cars. In 1992, the company **decided** to make the ultimate supercar. The result was the F1. It was the first car costing $1 million—and the fastest car on the road.

DID YOU KNOW?

An annual service for the McLaren F1 costs an amazing $35,000!

The back of the car is taken up by the huge BMW engine. It powers the F1 to 100 mph (161km/h) two seconds faster than a Ferrari and on to a blistering 240 mph (386km/h).

CARS

The F1's central driving position is unusual for a supercar. The two rear seats are also not common in a sports car.

STATS AND FACTS

LAUNCHED: *1992*

ORIGIN: *United Kingdom*

ENGINE: *6.1L (6,064cc) 48-valve V12, midmounted*

MAX. POWER: *627 bhp (468kW) at 7,400 rpm*

MAX. TORQUE: *479 ft. lb. (649Nm) at 7,000 rpm*

MAX. SPEED: *240.1 mph (386.4km/h)*

ACCELERATION:
*0–60 mph (0–97km/h): 3.2 seconds
0–100 mph (0–161km/h): 6.3 seconds*

WEIGHT: *2,513 lbs. (1,140kg)*

COST: *$880,200*

A total of 106 F1 road cars were built before McLaren stopped making them in 1998. Each one took almost two months to build!

21

PAGANI ZONDA C12 S

This car was designed by an Argentine named Horacio Pagani. It is named after a wind that blows from the Andes Mountains in Argentina. The Pagani Zonda is an exclusive supercar. There were only 15 built in the first year.

DID YOU KNOW?

When you buy a Zonda, you get a pair of driving shoes made by the pope's shoemaker.

CARS

The Zonda looks like a fighter plane. It has a glass-roofed cabin, twin **spoilers**, and a rocket-style exhaust. The inside is made of aluminum, suede, leather, and carbon fibers.

STATS AND FACTS

LAUNCHED: 2001

ORIGIN: Italy

ENGINE: 7.0L (7,010cc) V12, midmounted

MAX. POWER: 562 bhp (419kW) at 5,500 rpm

MAX. TORQUE: 552 ft. lb. (749Nm) at 4,100 rpm

MAX. SPEED: 220 mph (354km/h)

ACCELERATION: 0–60 mph (0–97km/h): 3.7 seconds

WEIGHT: 2,756 lbs. (1,250kg)

COST: $413,500

The Zonda has no trunk at all! The only luggage space is behind the seats.

This C12 S 7.3 model has a massive 7.3-liter V12 engine. It is made by AMG, who makes racecar engines for Mercedes-Benz.

23

PORSCHE 911 GT2

On the outside, the GT2 looks like an ordinary Porsche 911 Turbo. But inside, all of the luxuries have been removed to make it drive like a racecar. There is harder **suspension**, a **roll cage**, special brakes, and a lot of extra power! The GT2 costs $42,000 more than the Turbo, but it is the fastest 911 ever built.

DID YOU KNOW?

The 2008 GT2 is the fastest road car in Porsche's history, capable of 204 mph (329km/h).

German carmaker Porsche claims that the GT2 will accelerate to 186 mph (300km/h) and brake to a stop in less than 60 seconds.

CARS

The rear wing and side panels have vents to cool the huge engine. There are also vents in the **nose** and slits on the hood. They direct air to cool the radiator and brakes.

STATS AND FACTS

LAUNCHED: 2001

ORIGIN: Germany

ENGINE: 3.6L (3,600c) 24-valve V flat 6 turbo, rear mounted

MAX. POWER: 455 bhp (339kW) at 5,700 rpm

MAX. TORQUE: 459 ft. lb. (622Nm) at 3,500 rpm

MAX. SPEED: 197 mph (317km/h)

ACCELERATION: 0–62 mph (0–100km/h): 4.1 seconds

WEIGHT: 3,175 lbs. (1,440kg)

COST: $152,300

The GT2 is ten percent more powerful and seven percent lighter than the 911 Turbo.

TVR TUSCAN

TVR is based in England. It has been making affordable sports cars for more than 40 years. In 2000, the company started selling the Tuscan. It made the car as light as possible and gave it a huge engine. The result is an amazingly fast machine that costs much less than its rivals.

DID YOU KNOW?

John Travolta drove a purple Tuscan in the 2001 movie Swordfish.

To get into the Tuscan, press a little button under the rearview mirror. To get out, twist a knob inside the car.

CARS

The roof and the rear window can be taken off and stored in the Tuscan's large trunk. There is even enough space left over for a couple of suitcases!

STATS AND FACTS

LAUNCHED: 2000

ORIGIN: United Kingdom

ENGINE: 3.6L (3,605cc) 24-valve V inline 6, front mounted

MAX. POWER: 350 bhp (261kW) at 7,200 rpm

MAX. TORQUE: 310 ft. lb. (420Nm) at 5,500 rpm

MAX. SPEED: 180 mph (290km/h)

ACCELERATION: 0–60 mph (0–97km/h): 4.4 seconds

WEIGHT: 2,425 lbs. (1,100kg)

COST: $55,200

The Tuscan's engine uses up most of the space under the hood. It powers the car to 180 mph (290km/h).

27

AIRBUS A380

DID YOU KNOW?

The A380-800F freighter is used to carry heavy loads. It carries up to 165 tons of cargo.

Ever since the first airplane took to the skies, aircraft have gotten bigger and bigger. In 1970, American company Boeing produced the enormous 747. In 2005, a new giant started flying, the enormous Airbus A380. It was built by European company Airbus.

The body of the A380 is deeper and wider than a 747. There are two engines on each **wing**.

Airbus's A380 is a double-decker plane, carrying passengers on two spacious decks.

AIRPLANES

STATS AND FACTS

LAUNCHED: 2005

ORIGIN: Europe

MODELS: Five passenger versions and the A380-800F for cargo

ENGINES: Four Rolls-Royce Trent 900 engines or four Engine Alliance GP 7000 turbofans, rated at 311**kN** (69,916 lbs./31,713kg) thrust

WINGSPAN: 261.7 ft. (79.8m)

LENGTH: 239 ft. (73m)

COCKPIT CREW: Two

SEATING: Up to 853

MAX. SPEED: 634 mph (1,020km/h)

MAX. WEIGHT: 650 tons

RANGE: 9,445 mi. (15,200km)

LOAD: Up to 853 passengers or 165 tons of cargo

COST: $212 million

The standard A380 has room for 525 passengers, traveling in economy, business, and first classes. However, seating is flexible, and some airlines choose all-economy seating and carry more than 800 people.

SR-71 BLACKBIRD

In 1960, the Soviet Union shot down a U.S. spy plane. After this disaster, the American military was ordered to make a craft that would never be shot down again. The result was the amazing SR-71, packed with cameras and **sensors**. In 20 years of dangerous missions, no Blackbird was ever lost in combat.

DID YOU KNOW?

The Blackbird once flew from New York City to London, U.K., in 1 hour 55 minutes.

AIRPLANES

The Blackbird was made in top secrecy. President Lyndon Johnson refused to admit that it even existed until 1964.

STATS AND FACTS

LAUNCHED: 1962

ORIGIN: United States

MODELS: SR-71A, SR-71B, and SR-71C

ENGINES: Two Pratt & Whitney J58-P-10s with afterburners, each providing 144.4kN (32,462 lbs./14,725kg) thrust

WINGSPAN: 55.58 ft. (16.94m)

LENGTH: 103.84 ft. (31.65m)

COCKPIT CREW: Two

MAX. SPEED: 2,250 mph (3,621km/h)

MAX. WEIGHT: 86 tons

RANGE: 3,000 mi. (4,828km)

LOAD: Sensors and powerful cameras

COST: $45.5 million

Each engine has enough **thrust** to power an ocean liner. The large spikes catch air to keep the plane balanced in flight.

The SR-71's airframe is made of a special material called **titanium alloy**. It protects the plane from the extreme heat produced from flying at such high speeds.

B-2 SPIRIT

Stealth technology has developed very quickly. By 1978, it was possible to design an aircraft that was almost invisible to **radar**. One of the most striking of these airplanes was the B-2. The first model flew in July 1989 and looked like it came from another planet.

DID YOU KNOW?
The B-2's skin is jet black and smooth. All the joints are carefully concealed.

The B-2 is really just a giant wing with sharp edges. The strange bulges hide the plane's engines, **cockpit**, and bombs.

AIRPLANES

The plane has just two crew onboard. The rest of the cockpit is taken up by computer-controlled flight equipment.

STATS AND FACTS

LAUNCHED: 1989

ORIGIN: United States

MODELS: The U.S. Air Force has 20 planes, all slightly different.

ENGINES: Four General Electric F118-GE-110 turbofans, each rated at 84.5kN (18,996 lbs./8,617kg) thrust

WINGSPAN: 172.01 ft. (52.43m)

LENGTH: 69 ft. (21.03m)

COCKPIT CREW: Two

MAX. SPEED: 630 mph (1,014km/h)

MAX. WEIGHT: 200 tons

RANGE: 7,644 mi. (12,302km)

LOAD: Up to 25 tons of many types of nuclear or conventional bombs, missiles, or mines

COST: $2.21 billion (in 1998)

The B-2 is packed with computers and heat- and noise-reducing technology. It is the world's most expensive aircraft. In 1998, each plane cost an amazing $2.21 billion!

33

B-52 STRATOFORTRESS

After World War II, the U.S. Air Force decided to create huge aircraft that would deter people from starting wars. They were called the B-52s and were monster eight-engine jet bombers. In 1952, the first of these giants took to the skies.

DID YOU KNOW?

There are six ejection seats on a B-52 in case of an emergency.

The B-52 has sensors that let the plane fly very close to the ground during combat missions.

AIRPLANES

This B-52D has eight powerful engines. Despite their size, they burn less fuel than those found on earlier models.

STATS AND FACTS

LAUNCHED: 1952

ORIGIN: United States

MODELS: XB-52, YB-52 (1952), B-52A to B-52H (1954–1965)

ENGINES: Eight Pratt & Whitney TF33 turbofans, each rated at 75kN (16,860 lbs./7,648kg) thrust

WINGSPAN: 185 ft. (56.39m)

LENGTH: 161 ft. (49.05m)

COCKPIT CREW: Six

MAX. SPEED: 595 mph (958km/h)

MAX. WEIGHT: 283 tons

RANGE: 12,566 mi. (20,223km)

LOAD: Nuclear or high-explosive bombs, cruise missiles, and a variety of guns

COST: $8.3 million

This B-52 is being refueled in flight. **Air refueling** allows B-52s to fly almost anywhere in the world.

35

EUROFIGHTER TYPHOON

European countries get together to develop new warplanes. For each partner, this is cheaper than developing an aircraft by themselves. The latest example is the Typhoon, developed by Great Britain, Germany, Italy, and Spain.

DID YOU KNOW?

The idea for the Eurofighter dates back to 1979. However, it was more than 20 years before the first Typhoon was built.

Only 15 percent of the outside of the Eurofighter's body is made of metal. The rest is mostly lightweight carbon fibers that let it cruise at high speeds without overheating.

AIRPLANES

The Typhoon has two engines. It also has a large triangular wing and small-powered **foreplanes** on each side of the nose. The Typhoon comes in one- or two-seat versions.

STATS AND FACTS

LAUNCHED: 2002

ORIGIN: Europe

MODELS: Single-seat and two-seat versions

ENGINES: Two Eurojet EJ200 reheated turbofans, each providing 89kN (20,008 lbs./9,075kg) thrust

WINGSPAN: 36 ft. (10.95m)

LENGTH: 52.36 ft. (15.96m)

COCKPIT CREW: One or two

MAX. SPEED: 1,323 mph (2,129km/h)

MAX. WEIGHT: 23 tons

RANGE: 1,800 mi. (2,897km)

LOAD: One 27-mm gun (not used by the U.K.) and up to nine tons of missiles or bombs on 13 attachments

COST: $27.5 million

The twin engines allow the Typhoon to accelerate to **Mach** 1—the speed of sound—in under 30 seconds. The Typhoon can also take off in only five seconds!

F-117A NIGHTHAWK

First flown in 1981, the F-117A is perhaps the strangest aircraft ever made. Its shape is designed to break up enemy radar signals. Because it can be refueled in the air, the F-117A can travel almost anywhere in the world. This amazing plane was made by U.S. company Lockheed Martin.

DID YOU KNOW?
The only nonblack parts of the F-117A are the windows.

The F-117A is made up of hundreds of flat surfaces. These deflect enemy radar and make the plane almost invisible.

AIRPLANES

The F-117A is not really a fighter plane but a bomber. It carries its weapons inside, behind doors with zigzag edges. They open and close very quickly to release bombs.

STATS AND FACTS

LAUNCHED: 1981

ORIGIN: United States

MODELS: Five prototypes and 59 production aircraft

ENGINES: Two General Electric F404-F1D2 special turbofans, each giving 48kN (10,790 lbs./4,895kg) thrust

WINGSPAN: 43.3 ft. (13.2m)

LENGTH: 65.88 ft. (20.08m)

COCKPIT CREW: One

MAX. SPEED: 700 mph (1,127km/h)

MAX. WEIGHT: 26.2 tons

RANGE: Without air refueling, around 1,500 mi. (2,414km)

LOAD: Usually two 2,000-lb. (907-kg) laser-guided bombs

COST: $103.2 million

There are four F-117As on display in the U.S. One is on view to the public at the National Museum of the Air Force in Ohio. You can walk right up to this incredible airplane.

HARRIER

By the end of the 1950s, air forces started asking for planes that could operate from backyards, forest clearings, or even small ships. To meet this need, Hawker Aircraft in England launched one of the first **VTOL** (vertical takeoff and landing) aircraft in 1969. This plane was called the Harrier.

DID YOU KNOW?
The U.S. Marine Corps uses the Harrier to provide air power for a force invading an enemy shore.

This single-seat Sea Harrier operated from ships. There are also two-seat and trainer versions.

AIRPLANES

Harriers have a special system called **VIFF** (vectoring in forward flight). It lets them perform complicated maneuvers to confuse enemy fighter pilots.

STATS AND FACTS

LAUNCHED: 1969

ORIGIN: United Kingdom

MODELS: Seven versions

ENGINE: One Rolls-Royce Pegasus vectored-thrust turbofan, giving 84.5kN (18,996 lbs./8,617kg) thrust

WINGSPAN: 43.3 ft. (13.2m)

LENGTH: 46.3 ft. (14.1m)

COCKPIT CREW: One or two

MAX. SPEED: 700 mph (1,127km/h)

MAX. WEIGHT: 15.4 tons

RANGE: Without air refueling, around 1,700 mi. (2,736km)

LOAD: Missiles, rockets, and bombs

COST: $55 million

The engine has two nozzles on each side. They blast to the rear for high speed, downward for takeoff and landing, or forward to slow down.

41

JOINT STRIKE FIGHTER

In 1995, the U.S. Air Force and Navy launched a program for a JSF (joint strike fighter). Their goal was to produce the next generation of advanced planes for airfields and aircraft carriers.

DID YOU KNOW?

In 2001, the F-35 entered into a ten-year system development and demonstration phase.

All JSF models carry weapons in two bays on each side of the **fuselage**.

AIRPLANES

The rear exhaust produces thrust to lift the aircraft. The F-35B is given extra lift by a fan that takes power from the engine.

STATS AND FACTS

LAUNCHED: 2006

ORIGIN: United States

MODELS: F-35A, F-35B, and F-35C, described below

ENGINES: One Pratt & Whitney F135 turbofan, delivering 178kN (40,016 lbs./18,151kg) thrust, with one Rolls-Royce Allison engine-driven lift fan on the F-35B

WINGSPAN: Up to 43.5 ft. (13.26m)

LENGTH: 50.49 ft. (15.39m)

COCKPIT CREW: One

MAX. SPEED: 1,058 mph (1,703km/h)

MAX. WEIGHT: 30 tons

RANGE: Around 1,380 mi. (2,221km)

LOAD: An enormous variety of guns, missiles, and bombs up to 8.5 tons

COST: $91 million

There are three versions of the JSF. The F-35A is the basic version. The F-35B comes with a more powerful engine. The F-35C (*left*) has a bigger wing that can fold.

SPACE SHUTTLE

The first space flights relied on rockets—giant tubes that stood upright and were fired into orbit. In April 1981, the space shuttle was launched. It was the first spacecraft that could be brought back to Earth.

DID YOU KNOW?

The shuttle's boosters fall off into the sea. They are recovered and used again.

At the front is an area for up to ten crew, including two **pilots**. In the middle is a large **bay** for **satellites**. At the back are three big rocket **engines**.

AIRPLANES

Before launch, the **orbiter** is fixed on a huge tank holding liquid oxygen and liquid hydrogen. Attached to each side is a solid rocket booster.

STATS AND FACTS

LAUNCHED: 1981

ORIGIN: United States

MODELS: Columbia, Challenger, Discovery, Atlantis, Enterprise, Endeavour

ENGINES: Three orbiter engines with a combined thrust of 5,300kN (1,191,487 lbs./540,500kg), plus two solid rocket boosters with a combined thrust of 25.6**MN** (5,755,109 lbs./2,610,474kg)

WINGSPAN: 78 ft. (23.79m)

LENGTH: 184.19 ft. (56.14m)

CREW: Up to ten

MAX. SPEED: 17,439 mph (28,066km/h)

MAX. WEIGHT: 2,300 tons

RANGE: 116–403 mi. (187–649km)

LOAD: Satellites, components for the joint space station, and space experiments

COST: $1.73 billion, plus $406 million for each launch

After the mission, the shuttle returns to Earth. It is protected by heat-resistant tiles. The shuttle glides without engine power onto a runway and is slowed down by a large **parachute**.

VOYAGER

On December 23, 1986, a strange-looking airplane landed at Edwards Air Force Base in Mojave, California. It had taken off from the same runway nine days previously and flown around the world nonstop. This had never been done before.

Voyager was flown by two people. They had to lie down in a tiny space with a **propeller** at each end. The body of the plane was attached to the center of the amazing wings.

DID YOU KNOW?

During its epic journey, Voyager covered 24,986 mi. (40,211km) nonstop.

AIRPLANES

Voyager was made from carbon fibers and **glass fibers**. At rest, its wings scraped the ground, but in flight they curved upward like the wings of a bird.

STATS AND FACTS

LAUNCHED: 1985

ORIGIN: United States

MODEL: One

ENGINES: Two Teledyne Continental engines—front 130 bhp (97kW), rear 110 bhp (82kW)

WINGSPAN: 110.8 ft. (33.77m)

LENGTH: 29.2 ft. (8.9m)

COCKPIT CREW: Two

MAX. SPEED: 122 mph (196km/h)

MAX. WEIGHT: 4.9 tons

RANGE: 27,455 mi. (44,185km)

LOAD: Two crew

COST: $1.38 million

Voyager was one of many strange-looking airplanes created by Burt Rutan. It was flown around the world by his brother Dick *(right)*, with copilot Jeana Yeager.

X-43A

DID YOU KNOW?

The X-15 came before the X-43A. It reached an unbeaten speed of 4,534 mph (7,297km/h) during several flights.

NASA (National Aeronautics and Space Administration) is best known for making space rockets. It also carries out important research into aircraft. The X-43A is one of the latest research planes. It is used to find the best shape to fly at very high speeds in the upper part of the atmosphere.

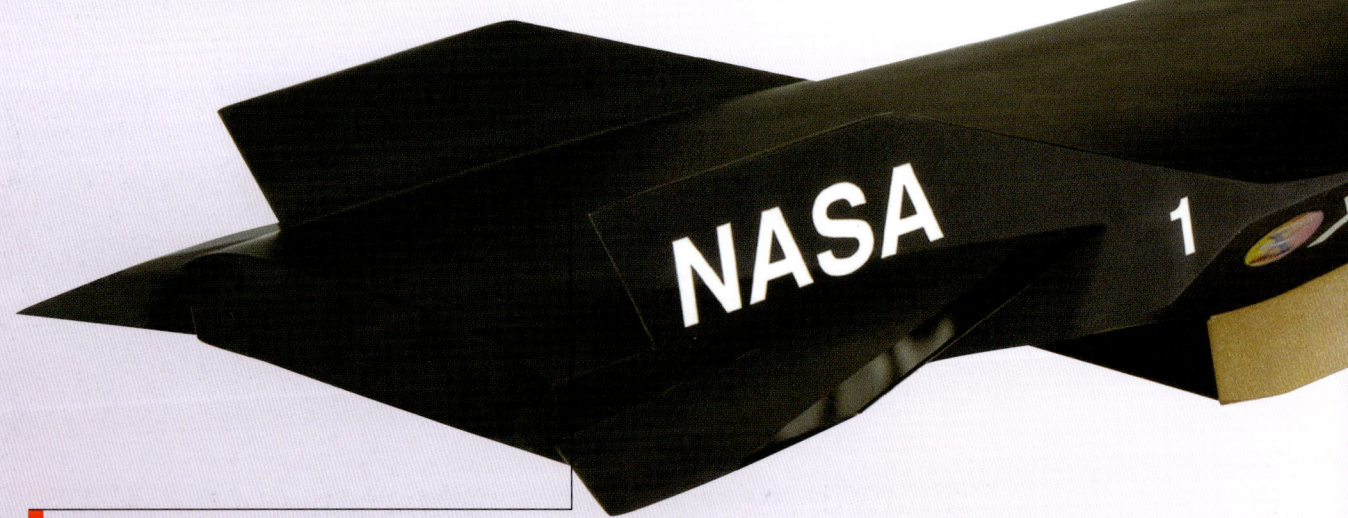

The X-43A has a wide bottom, flat top, and two fins. It is powered by a powerful **scramjet** engine, which burns hydrogen-based fuel.

AIRPLANES

After development, it is hoped that the X-43 will travel between Mach 7 and Mach 10, or 4,620–6,600 mph (7,435–10,621km/h). This means it will be able to travel from London, England, to New York City in only 40 minutes, a trip that usually takes seven hours!

STATS AND FACTS

LAUNCHED: 2001 (test version)

ORIGIN: United States

MODELS: Three test models, each slightly different

ENGINE: GASL hydrogen-fueled scramjet

WINGSPAN: 4.9 ft. (1.5m)

LENGTH: 12 ft. (3.66m)

CREW: Unmanned at present

MAX. SPEED: 6,600 mph (10,621km/h)

MAX. WEIGHT: 1.4 tons

RANGE: Unknown

COST: $347 million

The X-43A's first flight took place on June 2, 2001. It was dropped from a B-52 over the Pacific Ocean. After the boosters ignited, the X-43A did not follow its set flight path and was deliberately destroyed. It was found that the boosters' control system was to blame.

APRILIA TUONO FIGHTER

Italian company Aprilia first became known as a maker of bicycles. Then, in 1968, it began producing motorcycles and mopeds. In 2003, Aprilia launched the Tuono Fighter. This used many of the same parts as Aprilia's superbike RSV Mille R, of which there were only 300 made.

DID YOU KNOW?

Mille *is the Italian word for "one thousand." The RSV is called a "Mille" because its engine is almost 1.0L (1,000cc).*

The Tuono Fighter has special **radial brakes** at the front. These are much stronger than normal brakes, and the rider can stop very quickly if he or she needs to.

SUPERBIKES

One of the most eye-catching features of the Aprilia is its triple **headlight**.

STATS AND FACTS

LAUNCHED: *2003*

ORIGIN: *Italy*

ENGINE: *997.6cc V-twin*

CYLINDERS: *Two*

MAX. POWER: *123 bhp (92kW) at 9,500 rpm*

MAX. TORQUE: *74.5 ft. lb. (101Nm) at 7,400 rpm*

GEARS: *Six*

DRY WEIGHT: *408 lbs. (185kg)*

MAX. SPEED: *160 mph (257.5km/h)*

FUEL TANK CAPACITY: *4.8 gal. (18L)*

COLORS: *Red or gray (factory colors)*

COST: *$10,500*

The Tuono is equipped with a steering damper, which helps the rider avoid wobbling when traveling at high speeds.

BENELLI TORNADO

This Italian company was founded in 1911 by a widow named Teresa Benelli. She started the business to provide jobs for her six sons. The Benelli Mechanical Workshop started off making spare parts for cars and motorcycles. Then, in 1921, the company made its first motorcycle. In 2002, Benelli started selling the Tornado, a 163-mph (261-km/h) superbike.

The Tornado's engine is also used as part of the bike's **frame**. This makes the bike stronger.

DID YOU KNOW?

The Benelli is built in Italy, but it was designed by an Englishman and uses suspension made in Sweden.

SUPERBIKES

The Tornado's radiator is under the seat. Two big **fans** suck in air to cool it.

STATS AND FACTS

LAUNCHED: *2002*

ORIGIN: *Italy*

ENGINE: *898cc*

CYLINDERS: *Three*

MAX. POWER: *148 bhp (110kW) at 11,500 rpm*

MAX. TORQUE: *73.8 ft. lb. (100Nm) at 8,500 rpm*

GEARS: *Six*

DRY WEIGHT: *408 lbs. (185kg)*

MAX. SPEED: *163 mph (261km/h) (estimated)*

FUEL TANK CAPACITY: *4.8 gal. (18L)*

COLORS: *Green/silver*

COST: *$30,500*

A more powerful racing version of the Tornado has competed at the World Superbike Championship. It was designed by Italian Ricardo Rosa, who has worked with Italian car company Ferrari.

BUELL XB9R FIREBOLT

Buell was formed in 1993 by a man named Erik Buell. He set up the company with help from Harley-Davidson, a famous American motorcycle company. Harley-Davidson is not known for making fast bikes. But Buell had the idea of using a Harley engine in a lighter bike to make a really fast machine.

DID YOU KNOW?

Weighing only 386 lbs. (175kg), the Firebolt is one of the lightest superbikes in the world.

The Firebolt has a belt instead of a chain to make the back wheel turn around.

SUPERBIKES

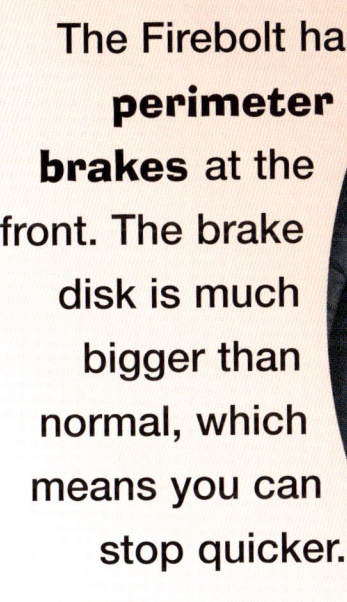

The Firebolt has **perimeter brakes** at the front. The brake disk is much bigger than normal, which means you can stop quicker.

STATS AND FACTS

LAUNCHED: 2002

ORIGIN: United States

ENGINE: 984cc

CYLINDERS: Two

MAX. POWER: 92 bhp (68.6kW) at 7,200 rpm

MAX. TORQUE: 67.9 ft. lb. (92Nm) at 5,500 rpm

GEARS: Five

DRY WEIGHT: 386 lbs. (175kg)

MAX. SPEED: 130 mph (209km/h) (estimated)

FUEL TANK CAPACITY: 3.7 gal. (14L)

COLORS: Arctic white, battle blue

COST: $10,200

The Firebolt has several unusual features. The tailpipe, which is usually on the side of motorcycles, is underneath it. The bike also has a hollow frame, which is used to store gasoline.

55

CAGIVA V-RAPTOR 1000

The Cagiva company built its first two motorcycles in 1978. One year later, it was building more than 40,000 bikes per year. This crazy-looking machine was designed for the company by Italian Miguel Galluzzi.

DID YOU KNOW?

The name Cagiva is made up of two letters each from the founder's last name and first name—Ca(stiglioni) Gi(ovanni)—and the first two letters from the company's hometown—Va(rese).

The Cagiva V-Raptor 1000 uses an engine made by Japanese company Suzuki. The "V" in the name describes the shape of the two **cylinders**.

SUPERBIKES

This bike has claws! The V-Raptor has a strange set of talons by the passenger footrest.

STATS AND FACTS

LAUNCHED: *2000*

ORIGIN: *Italy*

ENGINE: *996cc*

CYLINDERS: *Two*

MAX. POWER: *114 bhp (85kW) at 8,500 rpm*

MAX. TORQUE: *70.8 ft. lb. (96Nm) at 7,000 rpm*

GEARS: *Six*

DRY WEIGHT: *434 lbs. (197kg)*

MAX. SPEED: *149 mph (240km/h)*

FUEL TANK CAPACITY: *4.8 gal. (18L)*

COLOR: *Red*

COST: *$9,900*

The V-Raptor is "naked." This means that there is no **bodywork**, or **fairing**, covering the engine.

DUCATI 999R

DID YOU KNOW?
The "R" is based on the same bike that is raced in the World Superbike Championship.

Ducati is an Italian motorcycle company. The 999 comes in three versions—the 999, 999S, and 999R. The "R" is the fastest of the bikes and is made of carbon fibers and aluminum.

This is a Ducati 749. It looks almost exactly the same as the 999, but it has a 749cc engine. This means it has less power and is a little bit slower.

SUPERBIKES

The seat and fuel **tank** can be moved back and forth, and the footrests can be moved up and down. This Ducati can be made comfortable to ride, however tall or short you are.

STATS AND FACTS

LAUNCHED: *2002*

ORIGIN: *Italy*

ENGINE: *999cc*

CYLINDERS: *Two*

MAX. POWER: *139 bhp (104kW) at 10,000 rpm*

MAX. TORQUE: *79.7 ft. lb. (108Nm) at 8,000 rpm*

GEARS: *Six*

DRY WEIGHT: *425 lbs. (193kg)*

MAX. SPEED: *175 mph (281km/h) (estimated)*

FUEL TANK CAPACITY: *4.1 gal. (15.5L)*

COLORS: *Red or yellow*

COST: *$26,800*

Each 999R has a unique silver badge to prove that it is a limited-edition bike.

59

HARLEY V-ROD

Famous for being the bikes that Hell's Angels like to ride, Harleys have always been made for cruising. There are many straight roads in the U.S., and Harleys were made to ride long distances in comfort. However, the V-Rod is much sportier than other Harleys. It is the fastest bike that the company has ever made.

DID YOU KNOW?

Despite being a heavy motorcycle, famous stunt rider Evel Knievel did all his jumps on a Harley-Davidson.

The V-Rod's fuel tank is under the seat. The space this saves leaves room for **air intakes**. These force more fuel into the bike's engine, supplying the V-Rod with extra power.

SUPERBIKES

There is a special badge on the V-Rod's tank. It says that the Harley-Davidson company has been making motorcycles for more than 100 years.

STATS AND FACTS

LAUNCHED: 2002

ORIGIN: United States

ENGINE: 1.1L (1,130cc)

CYLINDERS: Two

MAX. POWER: 115 bhp (85.8kW) at 8,000 rpm

MAX. TORQUE: 64.9 ft. lb. (88Nm) at 6,300 rpm

GEARS: Five

DRY WEIGHT: 595 lbs. (270kg)

MAX. SPEED: 135 mph (217km/h)

FUEL TANK CAPACITY: 4 gal. (15.1L)

COLOR: Anodized aluminum

COST: $19,500

The V-Rod has a water-cooled engine. It was designed with German sports carmaker Porsche.

HONDA CBR1100XX BLACKBIRD

Japanese company Honda is one of the biggest motorcycle makers in the world. The Blackbird used to be the fastest motorcycle in the world, until Suzuki built the Hayabusa. With a few tweaks, the Blackbird can rocket to an incredible 200 mph (322km/h).

DID YOU KNOW?

In 2001, a rider on a turbocharged Blackbird did a wheelie at an amazing 200 mph (322km/h)!

The Blackbird has **linked brakes**. When you pull the front brake lever, the back brake works, too—and when you push the back brake pedal, the front brake works.

SUPERBIKES

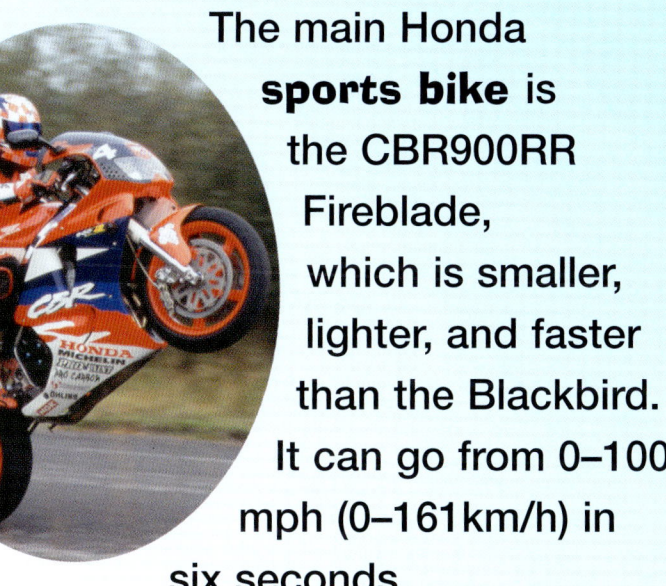

The main Honda **sports bike** is the CBR900RR Fireblade, which is smaller, lighter, and faster than the Blackbird. It can go from 0–100 mph (0–161km/h) in six seconds.

STATS AND FACTS

LAUNCHED: *1996*

ORIGIN: *Japan*

ENGINE: *1.1L (1,137cc)*

CYLINDERS: *Four*

MAX. POWER: *164 bhp (122kW) at 9,200 rpm*

MAX. TORQUE: *85.6 ft. lb. (116Nm) at 7,300 rpm*

GEARS: *Six*

DRY WEIGHT: *492 lbs. (223kg)*

MAX. SPEED: *174 mph (280km/h)*

FUEL TANK CAPACITY: *6.3 gal. (24L)*

COLORS: *Black, blue, red*

COST: *$14,400*

The Blackbird's **acceleration** is awesome. Due to its streamlined shape and huge engine, this bike can race from 0–130 mph (0–209km/h) in only 11 seconds.

KAWASAKI NINJA ZX-12R

Japanese company Kawasaki has always made very fast motorcycles. The ZX-12R is capable of just under 200 mph (320km/h). The Ninja also has a big fuel tank, which means you can ride it long distances without stopping.

The ZX-12R has such good brakes that it is able to go from 70 mph (113km/h) to a stop in under four seconds.

The scoop under the headlight forces air into the engine, which drags extra fuel in. This gives the ZX-12R even more power.

SUPERBIKES

DID YOU KNOW?
From 2001, speed limiters were introduced, reducing the top speed of the ZX-12R to 186 mph (300km/h).

STATS AND FACTS

LAUNCHED: 2000

ORIGIN: Japan

ENGINE: 1.2L (1,199cc)

CYLINDERS: Four

MAX. POWER: 165 bhp (123kW) at 9,800 rpm

MAX. TORQUE: 95.9 ft. lb. (130Nm) at 7,800 rpm

GEARS: Six

DRY WEIGHT: 463 lbs. (210kg)

MAX. SPEED: 190 mph (305km/h)

FUEL TANK CAPACITY: 5.3 gal. (20L)

COLORS: Black/gold, silver, Kawasaki green

COST: $13,000

The ZX-12R's fairing was made with help from Kawasaki's aircraft division. It was designed to make the bike as aerodynamic as possible.

MV AGUSTA F4 SPR SENNA

MV Agusta is another Italian company with a racing history. Agusta bikes won 270 Grand Prix between 1950–1975 before the company ran out of money and closed. Then, in 1999, MV Agusta was brought back to life with the launch of the stunning F4. Many people think the Senna is the most beautiful bike in the world.

The Senna's **exhausts** come out under the seat rather than at the side of the bike.

DID YOU KNOW?

Whenever a MV F4 Senna was sold, some of the money was given to educate Brazilian children.

SUPERBIKES

The Senna's twin headlights are arranged on top of each other. This makes the front of the bike more aerodynamic.

STATS AND FACTS

LAUNCHED: 2002

ORIGIN: Italy

ENGINE: 749cc

CYLINDERS: Four

MAX. POWER: 140 bhp (104kW) at 12,600 rpm

MAX. TORQUE: 59.7 ft. lb. (81Nm) at 10,500 rpm

GEARS: Six

DRY WEIGHT: 415 lbs. (188kg)

MAX. SPEED: 177 mph (285km/h)

FUEL TANK CAPACITY: 5.3 gal. (20L)

COLORS: Gray/red

COST: $24,100

The Senna was made in memory of famous Formula One driver Ayrton Senna. Only 300 were made.

SUZUKI GSX1300R HAYABUSA

Japanese motorcycle maker Suzuki was formed in 1952. In 1998, it built a new motorcycle called the Hayabusa. At the time, the Hayabusa was the fastest bike in the world. This monster's engine is actually bigger than those found in many cars.

DID YOU KNOW?
A Hayabusa is so powerful that it can wear out a back tire in as little as 1,000 mi. (1,600km).

The GSXR100 is the smaller brother of the Hayabusa. Its top speed is the same as the Hayabusa, but this bike has better acceleration because it is lighter.

SUPERBIKES

The British land-speed record for a motorcycle is held by a turbocharged Hayabusa. This bike reached a speed in excess of 257.4 mph (414.3km/h)!

STATS AND FACTS

LAUNCHED: *1998*

ORIGIN: *Japan*

ENGINE: *1.3L (1,298cc)*

CYLINDERS: *Four*

MAX. POWER: *156 bhp (116kW) at 9,000 rpm*

MAX. TORQUE: *98.8 ft. lb. (134Nm) at 6,800 rpm*

GEARS: *Six*

DRY WEIGHT: *474 lbs. (215kg)*

MAX. SPEED: *186 mph (299km/h)*

FUEL TANK CAPACITY: *4.8 gal. (18L)*

COLORS: *Blue/black, blue/silver, silver*

COST: *$11,500*

The hayabusa is a Japanese bird of prey that eats blackbirds. Suzuki called its new superbike *Hayabusa* because it is faster and more powerful than Honda's CBR1100XX Blackbird, its main rival.

YAMAHA YZF-R1

Yamaha Motor Company is one of the best-known motorcycle producers in the world. Originally a maker of musical instruments, the company started to make motorcycles after World War II. In 2002, Yamaha launched the latest version of its incredibly successful R1 bike, which has competed in the British Superbike Championship.

DID YOU KNOW?

The Yamaha R1 does more than 75 mph (120km/h) in first gear and more than 100 mph (160km/h) in second gear.

The R1 has no light bulbs at the back. Instead, it is equipped with tiny **LEDs** (light-emitting diodes). If one stops working, there are still another 20 to provide light.

SUPERBIKES

One of Yamaha's most popular bikes is the YZF-R6. It isn't as fast as an R1, but because it is small and light, it can keep up with most bigger bikes on twisting racetracks and roads.

STATS AND FACTS

LAUNCHED: 1998

ORIGIN: Japan

ENGINE: 998cc

CYLINDERS: Four

MAX. POWER: 152 bhp (113kW) at 10,500 rpm

MAX. TORQUE: 78.9 ft. lb. (107Nm) at 8,500 rpm

GEARS: Six

DRY WEIGHT: 384 lbs. (174kg)

MAX. SPEED: 176 mph (283km/h)

FUEL TANK CAPACITY: 4.8 gal. (18L)

COLORS: Blue, red, white

COST: $12,700

To make the new R1 even faster, Yamaha has given it a lighter **chassis** and wheels. The front and back of the bike are also more pointed and aerodynamic.

CALIFORNIA QUAKE DRAG BOAT

The fastest speedboats on the water are drag boats. These single-seat craft surge like rockets at breathtaking speeds over the waves, often spending more time above the surface than on it. This incredible machine has reached speeds of around 230 mph (370km/h)!

DID YOU KNOW?
Drag-boat racing attracts crowds of up to one million people.

The California Quake's 5,000 **hp** (3,729kW) engine meant it became the first boat to race 0.25 mi. (0.4km) in less than five seconds—a world record!

BOATS

Bottled air is supplied to the driver's helmet. This is so that in the event of an accident, he or she can continue breathing while waiting for rescue divers.

STATS AND FACTS

LAUNCHED: 1999

ORIGIN: United States

ENGINE: 8.2L (8,194cc) nitromethane engine, generating 5,000 hp (3,729kW)

LENGTH: 25 ft. (7.62m)

WIDTH: 12.2 ft. (3.72m)

MAX. SPEED: 198 knots (230 mph/370km/h)

MAX. WEIGHT: 5.3 tons

LOAD: One pilot

FUEL CAPACITY: 5.3 gal. (20L)

COST: $84,300

The most important part of the boat is the safety capsule. Complete with a roll cage, it breaks free from the boat in the event of a high-speed accident.

DEEP FLIGHT SUBMERSIBLE

Submersibles are like miniature submarines. They are used for deep-sea exploration. *Deep Flight I* is a tiny one-person submersible that does not use **buoyancy** (air/water) tanks. Instead, it has short wings that let it "fly" through the water.

The main body is made of a lightweight material that is strong enough to resist the high pressure of water outside the submersible.

DID YOU KNOW?

A trip in a submersible down to the sunken wreck of the giant liner Titanic *costs around $35,000.*

BOATS

Deep Flight I has a pair of stubby wings. Unlike the wings on an airplane, however, they pull *Deep Flight I* down through the water instead of up off the ground.

STATS AND FACTS

LAUNCHED: 1996

ORIGIN: United States

ENGINES: Two electric motors powered by ten 12-volt lead acid batteries, each generating 5.4 hp (4kW)

LENGTH: 13 ft. (4m)

WIDTH: 8 ft. (2.4m)

MAX. SPEED: 12 knots (13.8 mph/22.2km/h)

MAX. WEIGHT: 1.4 tons

ASCENT RATE: 650 ft. (198m) per minute

DESCENT RATE: 492 ft. (150m) per minute

LOAD: One pilot

COST: $1.5 million

Deep Flight I is equipped with up to four cameras and six lights. These are needed because the deep sea is completely dark.

ILLBRUCK RACING YACHT

Every year, the fastest yachts in the world get together for the Whitbread Round the World Yacht Race. In 2002, it was won by *illbruck*. The eight yachts in the competition covered more than 37,000 mi. (59,500km) in total, taking almost nine months.

DID YOU KNOW?

The entire illbruck *project—yacht, crew, backup team, equipment, training, transportation, and supplies—cost almost $23 million.*

BOATS

Around-the-world yachts battle giant waves, howling gales, collisions with icebergs, whales—and one another!

STATS AND FACTS

LAUNCHED: *2002*

ORIGIN: *Germany*

ENGINES: *n/a*

LENGTH: *64 ft. (19.5m)*

WIDTH: *17.22 ft. (5.25m)*

MAX. SPEED: *36.75 knots (42 mph/68km/h)*

MAX. WEIGHT: *14.9 tons*

LOAD: *12 people*

COST: *$22.5 million*

Crews pull the cables for the **sails** using high-speed **winches** with long handles. The height of the tallest mast is 85 ft. (26m).

The *illbruck's* satellite-communication center contains telephone, e-mail, and video-transmission facilities.

77

JAHRE VIKING OIL SUPERTANKER

The biggest ships in the world are the giant tankers that carry crude oil, or petroleum. Their precious cargo is used to make gasoline and other fuels, but also plastics, paints, and hundreds of other products. These huge tankers are bigger than islands and take 5 mi. (8km) to slow down and stop!

DID YOU KNOW?

The Jahre Viking *was bought in 2004 and renamed the* Knock Nevis. *It is now a permanently moored storage container.*

Most of the ship is controlled by computer. The crew is usually around 35–40. They control the vessel and live in the comparatively small **stern** section of the ship.

BOATS

Oil is pumped onboard through pipes at the oil terminal or rig. It is pumped off again at a **refinery**.

STATS AND FACTS

LAUNCHED: 1979

ORIGIN: Japan

ENGINES: Four steam turbines, each generating 50,019 hp (37,300kW)

LENGTH: 1,503 ft. (458m)

WIDTH: 226 ft. (69m)

MAX. SPEED: 10 knots (11.5 mph/18.5km/h)

MAX. WEIGHT: 714,248 tons fully laden, 622,545 tons unladen

CREW: 35–40 people

LOAD: 4.2 million barrels of oil

FUEL CAPACITY: 5,300 gal. (20,000L)

COST: $87.8 million

The entire **deck** area is as large as four football fields. It takes several minutes to walk the length of the deck, so crew members sometimes use bicycles to get around!

79

JAMES CLARK ROSS RESEARCH SHIP

One of the world's toughest ships, the *James Clark Ross* can smash its way through ice more than 6.6 ft. (2m) thick. This vessel is actually a huge floating laboratory, used for exploring and carrying out scientific research in the freezing waters of Antarctica.

There are five main sets of laboratories and science rooms onboard the *James Clark Ross*. More can be loaded onto the deck in house-size containers.

The main **hull** is extra strong. It is made of very thick **steel**, capable of pushing through ice and fending off icebergs.

BOATS

DID YOU KNOW?

A compressed-air system prevents ice from squeezing and cracking the hull by rolling the ship from side to side.

STATS AND FACTS

LAUNCHED: 1990

ORIGIN: United Kingdom

ENGINES: Two Wärtsilä R32 engines (3.1mW) and two Wärtsilä R22 engines (1mW), each delivering 8,500 hp (6,340kW)

LENGTH: 325 ft. (99m)

WIDTH: 61.84 ft. (18.85m)

MAX. SPEED: 15.7 knots (18 mph/29km/h)

MAX. WEIGHT: 6,319 tons

LOAD: 12 officers, 15 crew, one doctor, 31 scientists (maximum)

FUEL CAPACITY: 356,600 gal. (1,350,000L)

COST: $52.7 million

James Clark Ross surveys the oceans and measures depths and currents. It also acts as a floating weather station and even searches for strange creatures of the deep.

LOS ANGELES FIREBOAT NO. 2

Although ships are surrounded by water, they sometimes catch on fire. Their engines and fuel may go up in flames or they might carry cargo like oil, which can burn. Almost every big port has fireboats on hand to tackle emergencies. This vessel is one of the Los Angeles Fire Department's five fireboats.

DID YOU KNOW?

Firefighters wear breathing kits. This is because some types of poisonous smoke can kill in only a few seconds.

All parts of the fireboat are flameproof, in case there is an explosion of burning fuel nearby.

BOATS

When dockside buildings catch on fire, it is time to call in the fireboats. As well as fighting ordinary fires, they can tackle electrical blazes by spraying special foam rather than water.

STATS AND FACTS

LAUNCHED: *1925*

ORIGIN: *United States*

ENGINES: *Two 700 hp (522kW) V12 Cummins, three 380 hp (283kW) six-cylinder inline Cummins, and two 525 hp (391kW) V12 two-cycle Detroits, plus six engines for pumps*

LENGTH: *98 ft. (30m)*

WIDTH: *20 ft. (6m)*

MAX. SPEED: *17 knots (20 mph/32km/h)*

MAX. WEIGHT: *168 tons*

LOAD: *14 crew*

FUEL CAPACITY: *2,589 gal. (9,801L)*

COST: *$190,300*

Six powerful diesel-powered **pumps**, all with their own engines, suck in water from around the boat. Then they fire out powerful **jets** of water from water guns. These can reach heights of more than 492 ft. (150m).

NIMITZ-CLASS AIRCRAFT CARRIER

DID YOU KNOW?
Up to 20,000 meals are served every day to hungry sailors onboard the Nimitz.

Nimitz-class aircraft carriers are the biggest warships ever built. Each of these U.S. giants is a floating army, navy, and air force. The Nimitz-class has a crew the size of a small town, which includes 3,360 ship's crew and 2,500 aircrew. This number doesn't even include the soldiers and pilots!

This supercarrier carries up to 85 airplanes and six helicopters, along with all their spare parts, tools, pilots, and service crew. Jet fuel is stored in swimming-pool-size tanks.

BOATS

Supercarriers like the Nimitz-class aircraft carrier are equipped with the latest computers, radar, missiles, and other equipment. It takes three years to refuel, reequip, and repair these monsters.

STATS AND FACTS

LAUNCHED: 1972

ORIGIN: United States

ENGINES: Two nuclear reactors powering four steam turbines, producing 260,000 hp (194mW)

LENGTH: 1,093 ft. (333m)

WIDTH: 133.9 ft. (40.8m)

MAX. SPEED: More than 30 knots (35 mph/56km/h)

MAX. WEIGHT: More than 110,200 tons

LOAD: 3,360 ship's crew and 2,500 aircrew

COST: $1.8 billion

At 1,093 ft. (333m), the Nimitz-class carrier is almost as long as the Empire State Building is tall.

POLARIS VIRAGE TX JET SKI

The jet ski is a combination of motorcycle, water ski, and snowmobile. This vehicle is used for surging across the waves at high speeds. You can also do stunts on one—and even turn somersaults! If you lose your grip and fall off the craft, the water jet stops immediately.

DID YOU KNOW?

The jet ski was developed in the late 1960s. The idea came from American motorcycle rider Clay Jacobson, who was working for the Kawasaki motorcycle company at the time.

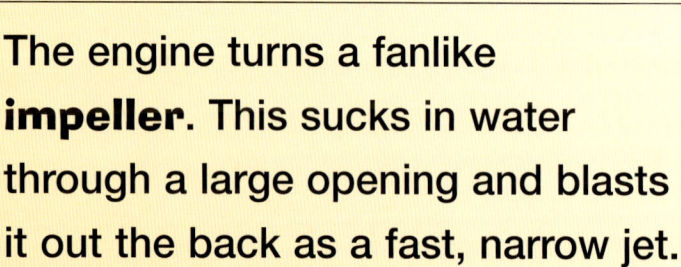

The engine turns a fanlike **impeller**. This sucks in water through a large opening and blasts it out the back as a fast, narrow jet.

BOATS

Jet-ski riders perform amazing turns, jumps, and loops. They can even dive completely underwater! In calm conditions, with little wind or waves, riders can reach speeds of almost 52 knots (60 mph/97km/h).

STATS AND FACTS

LAUNCHED: 2000

ORIGIN: United States

ENGINE: Polaris Marine 1200, producing 135 hp (100kW)

LENGTH: 10 ft. (3.06m)

WIDTH: 4.1 ft. (1.25m)

MAX. SPEED: 52 knots (60 mph/97km/h)

MAX. WEIGHT: 628 lbs. (285kg)

LOAD: One driver

FUEL CAPACITY: 20.3 gal. (77L)

COST: Up to $11,200

Turning the handlebars steers the jet ski left or right. Hitting "reverse thrust" pushes water forward and lets you brake or reverse.

THE WORLD LUXURY LINER

The World is a luxury **liner** with a difference—you live on it! For a vast price, you can buy a set of rooms onboard to make a permanent home. The ship travels to exciting world events, including the Rio de Janeiro carnival in Brazil and the Formula One race in Monaco.

DID YOU KNOW?

Rental costs for an apartment on **The World** *are between $2,000 and $5,000 per night.*

The 12 decks have every luxury you can imagine. There are seven restaurants, a casino, a nightclub, theaters, gyms, tennis courts, and swimming pools.

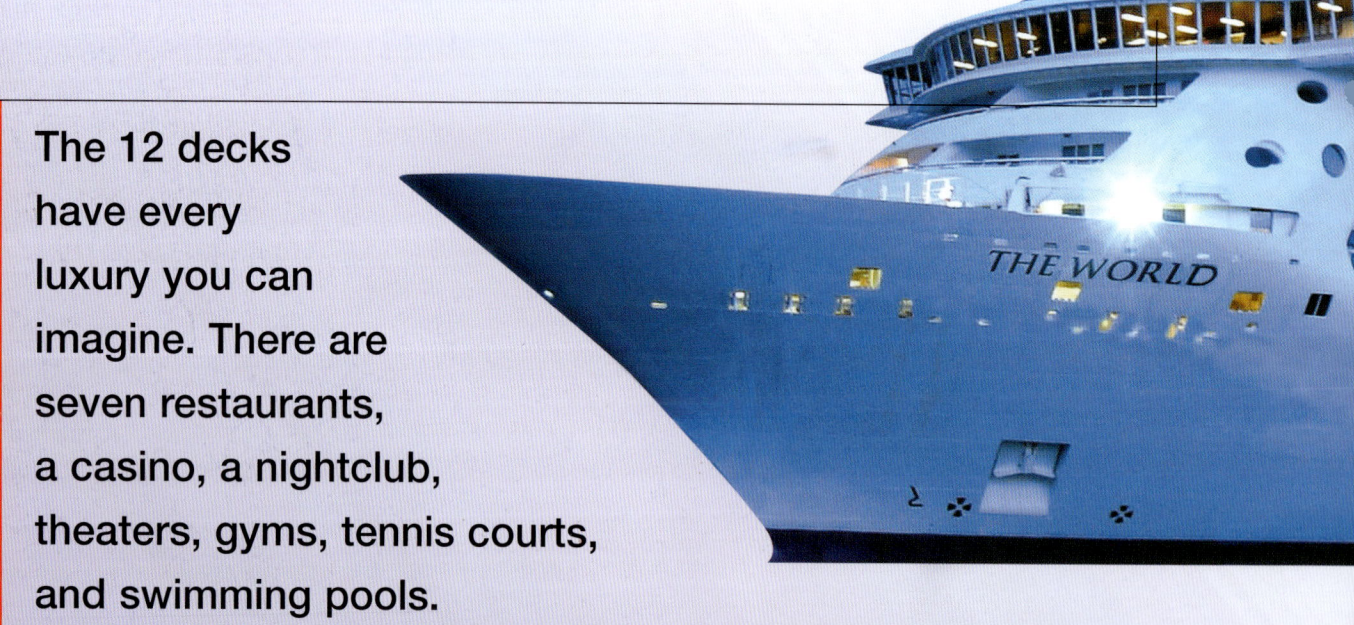

BOATS

On *The World*, people are not passengers but residents on a lifetime's vacations. There are 110 main residences, plus 88 extra apartments that can be rented out to guests.

STATS AND FACTS

LAUNCHED: 2001

ORIGIN: Norway

ENGINES: Two Wärtsilä 12-cylinder diesels, generating 7,402 hp (5,520kW)

LENGTH: 644.19 ft. (196.35m)

WIDTH: 97.8 ft. (29.8m)

MAX. SPEED: 18.5 knots (21 mph/34km/h)

MAX. WEIGHT: 47,977 tons

LOAD: Maximum of 976 residents, guests, and crew

FUEL CAPACITY: 303,800 gal. (1,150,000L)

COST: $230.3 million

The hull of *The World* was built using giant pieces of steel, lifted into place using huge cranes.

89

TRENT-CLASS LIFEBOAT

DID YOU KNOW?
In the waters around the United Kingdom, lifeboats are called out between 15 and 20 times each day.

Every sailor has two terrible fears— a shipwreck and drowning at sea. Brave lifeboat crews are always ready for rescue missions, and their boats must stay safe, even in the worst storms. The powerful Trent-class lifeboats are run by the United Kingdom's RNLI (Royal National Lifeboat Institute).

The hull of this lifeboat is made of various plastics, carbon fibers, and other **composites**. Unlike metal, these are lightweight but also very strong, and they never rust.

BOATS

Special radar and radio equipment can track ships in distress. This technology uses the Marsat and Sarsat emergency satellite-navigation systems.

STATS AND FACTS

LAUNCHED: *1994*

ORIGIN: *United Kingdom*

ENGINES: *Two MAN diesels, 808 hp (603kW) per engine, each around as powerful as a Formula One racecar engine*

LENGTH: *46.78 ft. (14.26m)*

MAX. SPEED: *25 knots (29 mph/47km/h)*

MAX. WEIGHT: *30.3 tons*

LOAD: *Six crew, plus ten survivors*

FUEL CAPACITY: *1,100 gal. (4,100L)*

COST: *$1.8 million*

The survivors' **cabin** has seats for ten people. There are also heaters, dry clothes, and a small **galley** serving hot drinks and snacks.

GLOSSARY

Acceleration The ability to make a vehicle go faster.
Aerodynamic Having a shape that cuts through the air around it.
Afterburners A system that injects extra fuel into the exhaust gases of an airplane to provide large amounts of extra power.
Air intakes Large scoops that direct air into an engine, sucking in extra fuel to give a motorcycle more power.
Air refueling A method of refueling military aircraft during flight via a fuel hose linked to a tanker aircraft.
Aluminum A lightweight, but strong, metal.
BHP Brake horsepower; a measurement of an engine's power.
Body The outer part of a car that covers the chassis and engine.
Bodywork The plastic panels that cover the chassis and engine of a car or motorcycle.
Booster A large canister containing fuel that is attached to the side of a space rocket as it is launched.
Brakes The parts of a vehicle used to slow it down.
Buoyancy The upward pushing force that water gives to objects, causing them to float if they are light enough.
Cabin An enclosed area on a ship, aircraft, or spacecraft that holds the crew, passengers, and cargo.
Carbon fibers Modern lightweight materials used to make many types of vehicles.
CC Cubic capacity; a measurement used for the size of an engine.
Chassis The part that holds the engine, wheels, and body of a car or motorcycle together.
Cockpit The part of an aircraft where the pilot and his assistants sit.
Composites Substances that are made of a mixture of materials such as plastics, metals, and fiberglass. Composites are usually very light and very strong.
Convertible See Roadster.
Coupé A two-door hardtop car.
Cylinders The parts of an engine where fuel is burned to make energy.
Dashboard The panel behind the steering wheel that usually contains the speedometer and other dials.
Deck The main floor or story of a ship, especially the uppermost flat area where people walk around.
Deployed Brought something into use.
Dynamic stability control A driver aid that can safely brake any or all four wheels.
Ejection seats Seats, usually installed in military aircraft, that can be fired or ejected from the aircraft.
Engine The part of a vehicle where fuel is burned to create energy.
Exhausts The pipes at the back of a vehicle where poisonous gases created when fuel is burned are let out. In cars and motorcycles, the exhausts are also used to reduce engine noise.
Fairing The front and side parts of the bodywork.
Fans The parts of a motorcycle that push or pull cool air through the radiator, helping cool the engine.
Foreplanes The movable surfaces at the front of an airplane that provide extra lift and balance.

Formula One A famous motor-racing championship.
Four-wheel drive A car that has power delivered to all four wheels.
Frame The part of a motorcycle that holds the engine, wheels, and bodywork together. Sometimes called the chassis.
Freighter An aircraft made to carry cargo rather than passengers.
Ft. lb. Foot pound—a unit used to measure torque. A foot pound is the torque that is generated by one pound of force being applied at right angles to a pivoting lever arm that is one foot long.
Fuselage The central body of an aircraft.
Galley The kitchen or dining area on a ship.
Gear A system that lets a car or motorcycle go faster or slower without damaging the engine.
Gearshift paddles The levers on a steering wheel used to change up and down gears.
Glass fibers Modern lightweight materials used to make many types of vehicles.
Headlight The bright light at the front of a car or motorcycle.
HP Horsepower; a measurement of an engine's power, originally based on the power of an engine compared to a horse.
Hull The main part or body of a ship, which floats on the water.
Impeller A fan-shaped propeller or screw in a tube that sucks water through the tube.
Jet A stream of fluid forced out under pressure from a narrow opening or nozzle.
Jets The parts of an engine that provide the lifting power for an aircraft.
kN (kilonewton) A unit of force equal to 1,000 newtons.
Knot One nautical mile per hour, equal to 1.15 miles per hour or 1.85 kilometers per hour.
kW (kilowatt) A unit of power equal to 1,000 watts.
LEDs Light-emitting diodes—the sources of light used in some brake lights.
Liner A large ship that carries passengers.

Linked brakes A system where the front brake lever also works the back brake and the back brake lever works the front brake.
Mach A measurement that relates the speed of an aircraft to the speed of sound. Mach 1 is the speed of sound (700 mph/1,127km/h). Mach 2 is twice the speed of sound.
MN Meganewton—a unit of force equal to 1,000,000 newtons.
Nm Newton meter—the unit used to measure torque. A newton meter is the torque that is generated by one newton of force being applied at right angles to a pivoting lever arm that is one meter long.
Nose The front end of a car or an aircraft.
Orbiter A spacecraft or satellite designed to orbit a planet or other body without landing on it.
Parachute A large canopy with a body harness underneath. It is designed to slow the rate of descent of a person from an aircraft.
Perimeter brakes A system where the brake disk is mounted around the edge of the wheel.
Pilots People qualified to fly an aircraft or spaceship.
Production car A standardized car that has been produced on a large scale.
Propeller A machine with spinning blades that provide thrust to lift an aircraft.
Pumps Machines used for raising water or other liquids.
Radar A system that uses invisible radio waves, beamed out and reflected back by objects as echoes. These are displayed on a screen to help identify other ships, planes, land, icebergs, and similar items.
Radial brakes A system where the brake disks are mounted at the bottom of the forks, parallel to the wheel.
Radiator A device through which water or other fluids flow to keep an engine cool.
Refinery A place where oil is turned into gasoline.
Roadster A car with a roof that can be folded back or removed.

Roll cage A metal framework within some vehicles that prevents crushing in the event of their turning over in an accident.
RPM Revolutions (of an engine) per minute.
Sails Fabric spread to catch or deflect the wind as a means of propelling a ship or boat.
Satellite navigation A system that tells you where you are by using satellites in space.
Scramjet A hydrogen-fueled engine designed for flying at five times the speed of sound.
Sensors Devices that help pilots fly their aircraft, detect enemy aircraft, or accurately fire weapons.
Spoilers The lightweight panels attached to a car to prevent the vehicle from lifting up at high speeds.
Sports bike A fast motorcycle that has been developed for road use.
Stealth technology The technology used to make an airplane almost invisible.
Steel A very strong metal.
Stern The rear part of a ship or boat.
Submersibles Boats that can function when underwater.
Superbike A fast motorcycle that is very similar to a race bike.
Supercar A fast, high-performance sports car.
Suspension Springs and shock absorbers attached to the wheels of a car or motorcycle, giving a smooth ride even on bumpy surfaces.
Tank A hollow metal unit where fuel is stored.

Targa A hardtop car with a removable roof panel.
Thrust A pushing force created in a jet engine or rocket that gives aircraft enough speed to take off.
Tire A rubber covering for a wheel filled with compressed air.
Titanium alloy A light, strong, and heat-tolerant material.
Torque The force with which engine power can be delivered to a car's or motorcycle's wheels.
Turbo A system that increases a vehicle's power by forcing more air into the engine.
V8/V12 The engine size given in number of cylinders.
Valve A device that controls the flow of gasoline into an engine.
VIFF Vectoring in forward flight. A system that allows an airplane to change direction very suddenly.
V inline/flat The arrangement of the cylinders in an engine.
VTOL Vertical takeoff, vertical landing. A system that holds an aircraft in the air as it takes off or lands.
Winches A system that lifts something by winding a line around a reel.
Wings The parts of an aircraft that provide lift, located on both sides of the fuselage.
Wingspan The distance between the tips of the wings of an aircraft.

INDEX

A
Airbus A 380 28–29
aircraft carriers 42–43, 84–85
air intakes 60, 92
air refueling 35, 39, 41, 92
aluminum 6, 17, 23, 58, 61, 92
AMG 23
Antarctica 80
Aprilia 50–51
Aston Martin 6–7

B
B-2 Spirit 32–33
B-52 Stratofortress 34–35, 49
badges 11, 18, 59, 61
belts 54
Benelli, Teresa 52
Benelli Tornado 52–53
bhp (brake horsepower) 17, 92
bicycles 50, 79
Blackbird (airplane) 30–31
Blackbird (superbike) 62–63, 69
BMW Z8 8–9, 20
bodywork 57, 92
Boeing 28
bombs 32, 33, 35, 37, 41, 43
Bond, James 6
boosters 44, 45, 49, 92
brakes 8, 24, 25, 50, 55, 62, 64, 92
British land-speed record 69
Brundle, Martin 16
Buell 54–55
Bugatti 10–11

C
Cagiva 56–57
California Quake drag boat 72–73
carbon fibers 14, 17, 18, 23, 36, 47, 58, 64, 90, 92
cargo 28, 29, 78, 82
Castiglioni, Giovanni 56
CBR1100XX Blackbird 62–63, 69
chassis 71, 92
Chevrolet 12–13
cockpits 32, 33, 92
compressed-air systems 81
computers 33, 78, 85
convertibles 13, 92
Corvette Z06 12–13
coupés 13, 92
crews 33, 44, 82, 84, 85, 90

D
dashboards 9, 92
decks 79, 80, 88, 92
Deep Flight I submersible 74–75
Die Another Day (movie) 6
drag boats 72–73
Ducati 999R 64–65
dynamic stability control (DSC) 8, 92

E
ejection seats 34, 92
engines (airplanes) 28, 31, 32, 34, 35, 37, 41, 43, 44, 45, 48, 92
engines (boats) 72, 82, 83, 86, 92
engines (cars) 8, 13, 14, 15, 20, 23, 25, 26, 27, 92
engines (superbikes) 50, 51, 54, 56, 57, 58, 60, 61, 62, 63, 64, 68, 92
Eurofighter Typhoon 36–37
exhausts 15, 23, 43, 55, 66, 92

F
F-117A Nighthawk 38–39
F4 SPR Senna 66–67
fairings 57, 65, 92
Ferrari 14–15, 18, 20, 53
Ferrari F50 14–15
Fireblade 63
fireboats 82–83
footrests 57, 59
Formula One 7, 14, 20, 67, 88, 91, 93
four-wheel drive 19, 93
frames 52, 55, 93
freighters 28, 93
fuel tanks 59, 60, 61, 84

G
galleys 91, 93
Galluzzi, Miguel 56
gears 7, 93
glass fibers 47, 93
Grand Prix 66
GSX1300R 68–69
GSXR100 68

H
Harley-Davidson V-Rod 54, 60–61
Harrier 40–41
Hawker Aircraft 40
Hayabusa 62, 68–69
headlights 6, 51, 64, 67, 93
helmets 73
Honda 62–63, 69
hulls 80, 81, 89, 90, 93

I
ice 80, 81
illbruck racing yacht 76–77
impellers 86, 93

J
Jacobson, Clay 86
Jaguar XJ220S 16–17
Jahre Viking 78–79
James Clark Ross research ship 80–81
jet skis 86–87
joint strike fighter (JSF) 42

INDEX

K
Kawasaki 64–65, 86
Knievel, Evel 60
Knock Nevis 78

L
laboratories 80
Lamborghini Murciélago 18–19
LEDs (light-emitting diodes) 70, 93
lifeboats 90–91
linked brakes 62, 93
Los Angeles fireboat No. 2 82–83
luxury liners 88–89

M
Mach (the speed of sound) 37, 49, 93
Marsat 91
McLaren F1 20–21
Mercedes-Benz 23
Miura 18
MV Agusta 66–67

N
"naked" 57
NASA (National Aeronautics and Space Administration) 44–45
National Museum of the Air Force 39
navigation 9
Nimitz-class aircraft carrier 84–85
Ninja ZX-12R 64–65

O
oil supertankers 78–79
orbiters 45, 93

P
Pagani, Horacio 22
Pagani Zonda C12 S 22–23
passengers 4, 28, 29, 89
perimeter brakes 55, 93
pilots 41, 44, 47, 84, 93
Polaris Virage TX jet ski 86–87
pope 22
Porsche 911 GT2 24–25
propellers 46, 93
pumps 79, 83, 93

R
racing yachts 76–77
radar 32, 38, 85, 91, 93
radial brakes 50, 93
radiators 11, 25, 53, 93
refueling 35, 38
research ships 80–81
reversing 19
RNLI (Royal National Lifeboat Institute) 90
roll cages 24, 73, 94
RSV Mille R 50
runways 45, 46
Rutan, Burt 47
Rutan, Dick 47

S
safety capsules 73
sails 77, 93
Sarsat 91
satellites 44, 77
satellite navigation 9, 91, 94
scramjet engines 48, 94
Sea Harrier 40
Senna, Ayrton 67
sensors 6, 30, 31, 34, 94
space shuttle 44–45
spy planes 30
stealth technology 32, 94
steel 18, 80, 89, 94
submersibles 74–75, 94
supercarriers (aircraft) 84, 85
supertankers (oil) 78–79
suspension 24, 52, 94
Suzuki 56, 62, 68–69
Swordfish (movie) 26

T
targas 13, 94
tires 6, 68, 94
titanium alloy 31, 94
Travolta, John 26
Trent-class lifeboats 90–91
trunks 23, 27
Tuono Fighter 50–51
turbo 56, 69, 94
TVR Tuscan 26–27
TWR (Tom Walkinshaw Racing) 17

V
V8 engines 8, 13, 94
V12 engines 23, 94
V12 Vanquish 6–7
VIFF (vectoring in florward flight) 41, 94
Voyager (airplane) 46–47
V-Raptor 1000 56–57
V-Rod 60–61
VTOL (vertical takeoff and landing) 40, 94

W
Whitbread Round the World Yacht Race 76, 77
windows 15, 27, 38
windshields 12
wings 10, 16, 25, 26, 43, 46, 47, 75, 94
World, The (luxury liner) 88–89
World Superbike Championship 53, 58

X, Y
X-43A 48–49
XB9R Firebolt 54–55
yachts 76–77
Yamaha 70–71
Yamaha R1 70–71
Yeager, Jeana 47
YZF-R1 70–71